Heart
ON HER SLEEVE

Heart on her sleeve
First published in Great Britain in 2024 by:
Enigma Press
An imprint of PARTNERSHIP PUBLISHING

Written By Amanda Crundall
Copyright © Amanda Crundall 2024

Amanda Crundall has asserted her right to be identified as the author of this Work in accordance with the Copyright, Designs and Patents Act 1988.
The editors have ensured a true reflection of the author's tone and voice has remained present throughout.
All rights reserved. No part of this publication may be reproduced, stored in a retrieval system, transmitted, or copied in any form or by any means, electronic, mechanical, photocopying, recording or otherwise, without the prior written permission of the publisher and copyright owner.

A CIP catalogue record for this book is available from the British Library.
ISBN 978-1-915200-64-8

Book Cover Design by: Partnership Publishing
Book Type Set by: Partnership Publishing

Book Published by:
PARTNERSHIP PUBLISHING
Lincolnshire
United Kingdom
www.partnershippublishing.co.uk

Printed in England.
Partnership Publishing is committed to a sustainable future for our business, our readers and our planet. This book is made from paper certified by the Forestry Stewardship Council (FSC), an organisation dedicated to promoting responsible management of forest resources.

Heart
ON HER SLEEVE

Amanda Crundall

ENIGMA
PRESS

My children: Zak, Erinn & Xander
My mother: Chris & my late step father Ray
Charlotte, Dean, Samantha & Terry

Contents

Foreword by Sarah Drury	1
Praise for Amanda Crundall	3

Part One: Depression

Blue Skies	7
Another Day	8
It's a year ago today	10
Vampires of the soul	12
Nightmare	14
Damaged hearts	17
No more tears birthday	18
Witching hour	19
Prozac	21
Festive blues	23
Love that never was	26
Salty tears	28
Thoughts	31
Clock ticks	32
Coffee for 10	33
I sometimes wish: part 1	34
The days in between	35
What will it be tonight?	36
Anxiety rising	37
Bully	38
Dead inside	39
Reaper	41
Belongingness	42
Hole in the heart aka cardiac rap	43

Monday blues	45
The mask of darkness	47
Home	49
Through the looking glass	51
Frozen	52
Detached	54
I sometimes wish: part 2	55
My hands are shaking	56
Broken dream	58
Bye Friday	60
Trauma bond	62
Shotgun	66
Alone	67

Part Two: Love and Life

The Phoenix	71
Sweet dreams	72
Autumn vibes	73
London bound	75
The end is near	77
Best friend	79
Feline company	81
Love me like this	83
Camping bliss	85
7 nights 7 days	87
Bot life	89
Get me off this railroad life	91
Hope	92
Lover	93
A solitary cigarette on Christmas Day	94

New Year	96
Shining through	98
Superego man	99
What are you thinking?	100
A fraction of a heart	101
Brown eyes	102
Half moon	103
Lovers in the moonlight	104
Random tears	106
Shining	107
Heart sparks	108
I want to start a rebellion	111
Lying here with you	112
Sober sex	113
The joy of laughing	115
You make me laugh	116
Chaos of kite	117
Frisky	118
Let's go camping	119
Red sky	121
Social butterfly	122
Blue moon	123
Cherub	124
Fucking hormones	125
New love	127
Seaweed life	129
Something silly	130
You see	131
120 Seconds	133
Step in my shoes	134
Pyjamas	137

When you think you'll never	138
My perfect place	140
Strangled by words	141
Frozen webs	142
Snowfall	143
The life to come?	144
I have done...	146
Paradoxical beings	147
Missing you	148
Ray's Poem	149
Acknowledgements	151
About Amanda Crundall	153

Foreword by Sarah Drury

I first met Amanda at Speak Out Scunny, a spoken word open mic in Scunthorpe. My first impressions were of a bubbly, positive, friendly lady with a quirky style and an air of panache.

Amanda takes the mic and whoosh!!! There she goes... A firecracker! A powerhouse of enthusiasm, putting her all into her poetry, with her burning commitment to deliver a stellar performance. She never fails to disappoint!

Being a full-time specialist nurse and a busy working mum does not deter Amanda from being immersed in the creative process. Whether it is writing, performing, or organising and co-hosting 'Rabbiting On', a spoken word event at the Rabbithole, (an independent bookshop in Brigg) she gives it 110%. She also involves her children in a multitude of creative events.

Amanda's poetry is emotive and almost confessional. As the title of the book suggests, she wears her heart on her sleeve! Her work encompasses a wide spectrum of emotional expressions, from heartbreak to joy, and all in between. Originally a cathartic process, writing has become her passion and main form of self-expression! Amanda has come home to her authentic self and found her voice! It is dulcet, expressive and resonates in the hearts of all who listen.

From the despondency of 'Dead Inside', with its opening lines of despair:

Dead inside
Charred
Chewed up by life
Chewed up by my mind

to the hopeful message of healing in The Phoenix:

The phoenix died but rose again,
The ashes warm with amber light,
The cry subsides, a voice is heard,
No more put-downs, no more fights,

Amanda's healing journey has brought fulfilment and gratification, channelling the supreme creative force that is pure love and inspiration.

I hope Amanda's poetry brings as much joy to the reader as it does when I am blessed to listen to her pour out her poetry in her authentic voice – full of joy, enchanting a captive audience.

Praise for Amanda Crundall

Powerful poems, some meant to be performed, some to be read. Plain written, uninhibited observations of the challenges of everyday life and the toll they take on our mental well being. A must read for the empath and the emotionally aware.

-Geoff Probert, Poet

Amanda Crundall is a very special poet. Not only does her work have great literary quality, written with wonderful rhythm and style but most of all, Amanda's words come from deep inside and she uses the heart as a beautiful symbol of human emotion. She explores the sadness, joy, despair and the great wonders of the roller coaster of that amazing thing we call life. If you ask me if I would recommend Amanda Crundall's poetry book, 'Heart On Her Sleeve,' then I would say "Oh yes, in a heartbeat…"

-Peter Cullum, Poet

Part One
Depression

Blue Skies

Beautiful blue skies
Rippled with ice cream fluff
The smile of young children
It needn't feel rough

Life, a series of chapters
That begin and then end
A new prologue is written
And new hearts are smitten

Beautiful blue skies
The sun shining through
Glistening on the ocean
Calming and still

Monologues, poems, sonnets
Broken hearts gently mended
Hearts so fragile
Bursting out with tears
Exposing our genuine childhood fears

Beautiful blue skies
Avoiding the storms
Life's not a goodbye
But breaking new dawn

Another Day

Another day
Another morning cup of tea
Blurry eyed
Exhausted by nightmares
When will it be over

Another day
Another bowl of porridge
Hand shaking with the spoon
Exhausted by terrors
When will it be over

Another day
Another school run
Scrambling for the keys to be on time
Speedy walk back
The workday begins
When will it be over

Another day
Another day at the home office
Distraction
So tired
Brave face
Gish smile
When will it be over

Another day
It's nearly Friday
But the kids won't be here
My babes will be gone
I keep busy
But I'm tired
I'm alone in my heart
My heart is broken
When will it be over

Another day
The darkness returns
I don't want the blackness
Not one bit
I dig deep
Keep strong I say to myself
Carry on
But I'm shattered
Both in mind and soul
When will it be over

It's a year ago today

It's a year today
When I told you to go
To leave quickly and pack your bags
and fly out the door

It's a year today
That I took the kids on holiday
Without you
It felt odd, to be honest
So much worry, so complicated
Love and feelings bubbling over
like a glowing cauldron

It's a year today
When I told you to go
The counsellor stopped that session
Your anger flaming – a blazing fire
that sadly will not be extinguished

Enough is enough
I tried so hard to make things work
Bent over backwards to help you
with your demons
You said you would change

I know now that will never happen
Nobody is right but you
I couldn't have friends easily
without petty jealousy

I couldn't have career success
without put-downs
I couldn't love my own children
without jealousy
Rising like a child
stamping dusty feet
I gave you everything, nearly my life

It's a year today
When I told you to go
It's been an enormously challenging one
Still not even fully divorced

Pfft

Now you can't control my life,
I know you still keep trying
Now I can love my children
Relax with ease
Now I can see *female* and *male* friends
God, yes, *male* friends
How we need both in our lives
Now I can be *ME*, just *ME* and pursue
My mothering and friendships
as I please

A year has passed, progress has been made
and this woman re-emerges slowly
Surely and stronger than ever before
I know we will never be left in peace
but my Teflon suit is getting a little
stronger every day

It's been a year, *today*

Vampires of the soul

They seek you out
You are strong
But they steal your blood

They seek you out
You are successful
You have an eternal life force, to feed them
They syphon your blood

They seek you out
Because you are everything, they want to be
They suck you dry

They seek you out
And make you cry
Again and again and again
You endure almighty pain

They seek you out
Your soul is beautiful
Slowly, slowly, slowly
It's chipped away

They seek you out
Jealousies bare
You should have no one, but them
You become - so scared

They seek you out
You're positivity drained
Your soul demented
You question your life
You question yourself, over and over again

Until, one day…
You find the strength to say
"NO MORE, NO MORE!"
You will not change, not ever –
This is not forever
NO MORE CHANCES
No more skirting between the dances,
The facade, the shitstorm of the whole
No more vampires of the soul

Those vampires feast all the while
You think they are gone
But they always lurk

Beware, beware, my soul

The vampires have been
So many times before

PLEASE!

No more vampires for this soul

Nightmare

Last night
You were there again
Haunting me
A true nightmare
Not able to wake
Not able to shout
Voiceless

Voiceless for years
A life lived on mute
Until I found
The max volume
The treble, the bass
The equaliser
And I spoke
I spoke

OUT LOUD

Last night
You were there again
Intimidating me
A true nightmare
Not able to wake
Not able to shout
Voiceless

A life controlled
A life put down
A life that brought me my children
My blessing
Not all a waste
Look for the positive

But you were there last night
Again
Shouting
That look, the flash
of uncontrollable anger
On edge all the while
Walking on broken eggshells

A complicated life
One that needn't have been
But this was a lucky escape
The haunting
The dust trying to settle
The haunting of life
Recurring, recurring
Most nights
Re-living a nightmare

Last night
You were there again
Been clever
A true nightmare
Not able to wake
Not able to shout
Voiceless

I live for those days without the terrors
I live for those days without the clever dick
I live for those days without the intimidation
I live for those days where I can wake
Without thinking about what next...
I live for my children and my new life

Let me sleep without fear
Let me sleep without fear
Let me sleep without fear

Damaged hearts

A heart is burned
Singed beyond compare
Lifeless, blackened with nothing to spare
A heart is taken

A heart is blocked
Furring arteries, cholesterol, and sludge
The pain needs morphine
It's so unbearable

New beginnings emerge
New friendships beckon
Positive, hope and happiness
May not be forgotten

The heart can spark chaos
Balloons, stents and electricity
And pumps needed to survive
That may just keep that heart alive

Anatomy and emotions intertwined
But different but the same in need of being hot-wired
So, the hearts that are singed, the hearts that struggle to pump
Can get there, I hope, with love, compassion and care
So, it needn't be endless and so utterly bare

No more tears birthday

Today, was a no-tears birthday!
I am thankful for that
Several birthdays before
have been full of tears

How sad eh
It may seem strange
But people are strange

So, no more tears
And this isn't a Johnson's advert!

Birthday 45 has been lovely
Time with my babies
And my mum
Out for brunch
And the sun shone

Simple pleasures
A birthday shouldn't be spoilt
By any other
Hard to understand
Why someone would do that

Anyway, my birthdays have been freed
And I can do with them as a please
No more birthday tears for me

Witching hour

When I was a proper nurse
The witching hour was mean
That 5 am till handover
Was such a fucking dream

So the witching hour now
Is that of a 'woe is me'
Well *fuck* that witching hour
That is so cruel to me

I think of you at night
It leaves me in a fright
Of what a life is ahead of me
My kids and the strife

I love you and I hate you
For what has happened thus
I really thought the way out
Was in front of that bus

But no, *fuck* no!
My strength within me shouts
What am I doing?
You, lousy, fucking lout

My kids are both amazing
Am I going crazy?!
Well, you know, you made me like that

You blooming twat
Oh my god, I love you!
How can I say this?

My heart is on a shoe string
And needless other things
My heart is truly broken
Why, oh, why, oh, why?
Did this have to be goodbye

Of all the things you've done
My heart remains enormous
So honest and so vulnerable
It's cardiomyopathic

Prozac

Prozac,
Fluoxetine,
Happy pill,
SSRI,
Boosting the brain when the cells collide

Prozac,
Fluoxetine,
Happy pill,
SSRI,
I met you once you made me smile

Prozac,
Fluoxetine,
Happy pill,
SSRI,
All that time ago when I was 25

Prozac,
Fluoxetine,
Happy pill,
SSRI,
I said goodbye in 2009

Prozac,
Fluoxetine,
Happy pill,
SSRI,
Well hello there, I'm not even 45

Prozac,
Fluoxetine,
Happy pill,
SSRI,
This time you didn't make me smile

Prozac,
Fluoxetine,
Happy pill,
SSRI,
Lifetime passing, reflections mile-high

Prozac,
Fluoxetine,
Happy pill,
SSRI,
Holy shit, how depressing

Prozac,
Fluoxetine,
Happy pill,
SSRI,
Why did this SUB become so repressing?

Prozac,
Fluoxetine,
Happy pill,
SSRI,
It's time to say *goodbye.*

Festive blues

It's December
Bang
It's busy
It's manic
Such pressure

It's December
Christmas films
Baileys
Cheese puffs
Chocolate fingers

It's December
Christmas 'dos' you still can't attend
Christmas lights
Christmas trees
Christmas decorations
Find the ladders

It's December
Children chatter
Build with excitement
Advent calendar not 1
But 2, 3, 4
For goodness' sake

It's December
Greed surmounted
In epic proportions
It's nauseating
Is there an escape

It's December
Failing relationships
Fester and fornicate
Because its Christmas
And everything is OK right?
Like a magician conjuring social media
Drivel all over, making people believe
There is this nirvana to be found

It's December
Jack Frost is whizzing around
Causing mayhem on the roads
Lockdown fall out on infection control
Bugs rising like red traffic lights on tongues
Children dying

It's December
It's nearly Christmas
That means everything will be OK doesn't it?
Or does it...?
Tempers flare, the cracks appear
Hearts look elsewhere
Brains are burnout
We look for escape

It's December time
It's that magical month

The one full of joy
The one full of sorrow
The one full of despair
The one full of festivity
The one that rocks so many worlds

Maybe, just maybe the world is rocked
A little too much already

It's December

Love that never was - Absent love

V1

I trusted you, you trusted me
I loved you but you didn't love me
Your tricks and games
Hurt me and my babes

Chorus 1

Gaslight here, gaslight there
Put downs, shutdowns
Jealousies bare
You just don't care

V2

The children wonder
What happened to daddy?
He chose the life
Not to be with any strife or happy

Chorus 2

Kids shut down here
Kids shut down there
So jealous and deceitful
You just don't care

V3

My empathy has killed me
My compassion worn
My heart so wounded
My face a telling stone

Chorus 1

V4

Oh, what have you done?
Oh, what have you done?
How foolish I've been
To love you and not another one

Chorus 2

Salty tears

Sat in the park the morning
after the packs of lies
Deceit came calling
and negativity back

Kids calling, playin'
in the background
I look at the world in front
and I wonder what my part
is, these days
Observations of others
Are they happy?
Are they sad?
Are they content?
Is anyone content?

Sat in the park, subtle
afternoon sun soothing my soul
The salty tears flow hidden
beneath my shades
Dripping down, a quick dab
trying to wipe the evidence
Away from children

Sat in the park, mental effort
of keeping calm
With forced, upturned smile
for the children
Exhausting me

Salty tears uncontrollable
Streaming: parents, grandparents
look at me
I lay down my head
on my knees,
hiding my face

My son sits by me
I've let him down
He shouldn't see this
He asks
'Who's hurt you mummy?
Is it to do with him, again?'

Silence
Silence
Silence

I wipe my tears
I say I'm sorry, and say,
'The world hurts sometimes, son'

Sat in the park, feeling alone
confidence attacked
Feeling like a failure
To my children
To my friends and family
To myself

Again
Again
Again

Sat in the park wondering
whether my time has come
to leave this painful world
But how much pain
I would cause my children

Trapped
Trapped
Trapped

Feeling like every last fragment
of me has been shattered
Now blowing away across the park
in the breeze like my ashes
that have arrived

Prematurely

Thoughts

You are my first thought when I wake
You are my last thought before I sleep
When will this change?
I ask myself every day

My mind wanders here
My mind wanders there
So annoyingly regular
Like clockwork

When will I stop this?
I really don't know
Troubles me over and over
Will it please just go?

I don't want to think of you
The pain is too great
I'm trying so hard to move on
Oh no, you're here again

Come on now I say
Let the thoughts drift away
It's just so endless
It seems they will stay

Please, leave me in peace now
Let my heart heal, my soul re-emerge
From the dark sinking feeling
Those inner thoughts need healing

Clock ticks

Empty house
The clock ticks
Brain's sick
Ticking bomb
Waiting to implode
Time to run

Coffee for 10

Head's in a rut
Mustn't let it get stuck
Come on, come on Mandy
Turn it around right now

Drink the coffee
Swallow the grains
Of mental plight
Don't spoil the time

Be present, be present
All the while
A mother's anguish never rests
Of what to come
She feels she cannot protect

I sometimes wish: part 1

I sometimes wish life was complete
A nail in a coffin
Or ash on the sea
Woeful self-pity
Oh, poor me

I sometimes wish life was far away
Warm sun, sand, and sex
and imaginative play

I sometimes wish life was endless spontaneity
Bouncing along, having fun
Not a care in the world
No special deity

I sometimes wish life was simple and just
Where being at ease is simply a must
Not harangued by thoughts twisting your guts
No ifs, no buts, just full of lust

I sometimes wish I didn't think,
Didn't ponder on thoughts so dark
But without the dark, the light never shines
And that, dear friends, is just fine

The days in between

The days in between
Sometimes so unbearably long
Heart pines
A life less sublime

The day then cometh
My day is brighter
My heart lifts
My eyes transfixed

The time then passes
The clouds return
The endorphins rush
I don't want to be pushy

But please
Take me in your arms
Hold me
Tight
Kiss me gently
And take away my fright

What will it be tonight?

Gin, diazepam, ciggy
Which one?
One, two, or all three

Gin, diazepam, ciggy
Uppers and downers
Or maybe an equal strategy

Gin, diazepam, ciggy
Maybe it's not such a biggie
But my brain's in meltdown

Gin, diazepam, ciggy
Life so confusing
I'm fed up with musing

Gin, diazepam, ciggy
Or what?
Maybe it would be easier
if I was an un-emotive bot

Anxiety rising

Anxiety rising – a volcanic eruption
Spewing out laval emotion
Streaming everything it touches
The earthly core revolting
As it simmers away

First quietly
Then bubbling
Until its orgasmic explosion
Ejaculating
Over everything in sight

From controlled to uncontrolled
From submissive to virile
From poetic to destructive
It reigns its terror
On that recovering mind

The calm then returns
At first wavering
Dipping in and out
The anxiety pulling, coming again
Then no more
No more

Bully

Tell me who hurts a child
Tell me who intimidates others
Tell me who patronises others
Tell me who blames others for their actions
Tell me who wants to control others
Tell me will they ever leave others in peace
Tell me who gaslights
Tell me who thinks the world revolves around them
Tell me who is omnipotent
Tell me who thinks they know best
Tell me who thinks children are second best
Tell me who's a red flag
Tell me
Tell me
Tell me

Dead inside

Dead inside
Charred
Chewed up by life
Chewed up by my own mind

Dead inside
Sometimes
Still triggered
Still hanging in there
Still hoping for respite

Troubled inside
Will it be fixed
Will it ever be over
Will I have peace

Peace inside
An unknown feeling
A girls name
A collection of irony

Empty mind
Empty heart
Broken
Broken
Like hundreds of shattered
slithers of glass

Sweep up the shards
Sweep away the piercing reminders
which puncture my heart
Sweep them away

Let it be done

Reaper

The reaper looks upon
Those dark minds
Entangles the scythe
Around those wounds
That cut so deep
So hard to heal
The unknown does not steal

The reaper hears you
The reaper listens
The reaper waits for you to join those
with journeys that have succumbed

The reaper ends the pain
No more hurt
No more loneliness
No more life
Because death has only just begun
Our song is now sung

Belongingness

What does it mean?
Feeling like I don't belong
Anywhere
To be honest

Belongingness
To belong
Not to belong
It's a question in sight

I look around
What do I see?
Society changing
This isn't for me

Walking around
Just the greatest misfit
A jigsaw with missing pieces
Or simply the wrong piece

Lost in a world
She doesn't understand
Looking for a world
That's truthful and bold

Belonging
Belongingness
To belong
Belonged to
What does it mean?

Hole in the heart aka. cardiac rap

Where the blood pours through,
mixing good with bad.
Where emotions run wild,
in the wrong sac.

Breathless and energy,
draining fast.
Competing with life-sucking emotions,
from the past.

Red blood or blue blood,
The life source competing,
Dementors floating,
Lifeforms fleeting.

Gasping for air,
Pallor's dismal.
The wanton of calmness,
The heart's hole abysmal.

What happens next,
Sewing up fast.
Maybe for the best,
For this grey patch.

Repairing gaping holes,
Of the de-generating souls.
Red bloods back,
Need to act fast.

Pouring
Feeling
Dreaming
Appealing

Life's what you make it.
Catch it if you can.

Monday blues

So tired
So blue
So frosty
Garden pretty
Thick with ice
Penetrating the mind

So tired
Standing on the doorstep
ECT effect
Jolting the cells so they don't collide
Ice bath maybe should be the next step

So tired
Brain wants to be at peace
Turning a new leaf
But the blue frost is there
I have nothing to spare

So tired
In need of thawing
No time for moping
Brave face
School run
Don't stop now
No need for a bow

So tired
Just keep on going
Ice will melt
Cells will reignite
One day
The sun will shine
My heart will melt

So tired
Just let me sleep
Let me have some peace
Let the darkness consume
The Monday Blues

The mask of darkness

The mask
The mask
The mask of darkness

Waiting
Waiting
Waiting for the day it hangs its soul

The paradox
The paradox
The paradox of the mask
That provides both comfort and a dark veil
in a bonkers world of task and function

Thinking
Thinking
Thinking of what troubles you most
when it should be parked by the host

Tortured
Tortured
Tortured minds
They feel they should be left behind

Left behind
Left behind
Left behind but that wouldn't be kind

Entangled
Enmeshed
Engrained
In the grey
In the white
matter

Journey
Journey
Journey on through this black hole
Alone

Home

This is their special place
Where love and peace prevail
A personal space – a retreat
when life becomes too great

A space of creativity
Where minds collide and gel
One that siblings can hide away
from the societal hell

Their love for one another
is the strongest bond I know
They may not always see eye to eye
but each other's formidable ally

Oh, I want what's best for you
My sweetest little loves
You don't deserve this hassle
The tussle, the bustle
of a topsy-turvy life

A life, that doesn't have the strife
We live not in fear of that control
No sledgehammer approach
Here, please our cup now overflows

So, leave them in their safe place
They have been through too much
Just put them first, always
That's what children deserve

We are there to protect them
To be their role model cast
To love them and to cherish them
Womb no more, they are exposed

A maternal drive that's fierce
One that never idles
One that will never stop
I will always love them the most

Through the looking glass

Take a good look in that looking glass
Who do you see?
Nothingness
Blackness, looking back at me

A lost soul
A tormented
Demented
Lost within the whole

A tired wanderer
Pondering the end
A weary cerebrum
Hoping there's an end

To the mental humdrum
The withering thoughts
The playing of games
Strewn across the lanes

Life is for the living
Not for the dead
This body is done
An empty shell

Take another look through that looking glass
What do you see?
A frail ageing soul
looking at me

Frozen

Frozen
So beautiful
Pretty icicle shards
Gentle snowflakes
Glinting in the white light

Frozen
Blood stiffening
Temperature cooling
Hands trembling
Trapped in an icy heart

Frozen
Majestic, frosty white landscapes
Romanticising their patterns for all to see
In the woods, in the park
upon the coastal promenades

Frozen
Hearts refrigerated
Closed
No entry
Frozen grief not budging

Frozen
Children combing up frost from cars
Eagerly waiting to see
If snow will follow
Laughing and writing messages
On car windows
'Jack Frost woz ere'

Frozen
Frozen hearts
Trying to thaw
Trying to defrost their core
The ice protecting and preserving
from further damage

Frozen lives
Frozen beautiful season
Frozen hearts
Let's melt a while
Can we trust this magnificent force
of nature and our true hearts?

In time and space and warmer climes
We will see what unveils the hearts
So brittle that could shatter like ice
The frozen icebreaker has never been
So welcoming.

Detached

Detached
Hovering above surroundings
Numb
Shut down
Feeling like a ghost floating above my own grave

Attached
Hanging on with a life less complex
Self doubt taking prisoners of war
Shutting down
In protection mode

Mind butchered
On the chilly ping of an email
Emotions wrung out in the spinner of disillusionment
On an cycle that never ends
Aghast, at the horror that enfolds

Detached
Hovering above surroundings
Frozen
Annihilation of the soul
Feels so normal or is that just another hole

Detached forever
Or
Freedom
From the tormented mind
To live, like is deserved for many

I sometimes wish: part 2

Sometimes I wish I could start all over
but I wouldn't have the people in my life now

Sometimes I wish I could rub out parts instead and
delete brain storage

Sometimes I wish I was never born
so the pain would have never existed

Sometimes I wish I could pack my bags
and never return

Sometimes I wish
Would someone just love me

Sometimes I think I am not worthy
and it's a waste of a journey

Sometimes I wish I wouldn't wake up
and sleep a while longer

Sometimes I wish I was dead
then the pain is no more

Sometimes
it's meant to be game over

My hands are shaking

My hands are shaking
Daft really
But my hands are shaking
With my cuppa this morning

Found two memory boxes yesterday,
In the kitchen cupboard
Full of cards, poems, ditties –
You name it,
From both sides, 11 years
Not sure what to do with them
Apart from burning them (to be honest)
But my hands are shaking

My hands are shaking
Daft really
Just stuff
But my hands are shaking
With my cuppa this morning

Funny, nostalgia isn't it?
Can catch you out
Wouldn't reverse my decision for a million
But it still brings sadness
And that hand-shaking
Is a mourning

My hands are shaking
With my cuppa this morning
My heart is racing
My head is pounding
My stomach churns

It's time for the burning

Broken dream

A tumbling feeling when your heart is taken by him,
Not a cog unturned, not a whirr is silenced,
The constant thoughts, the constant pangs of love,
Bursting open into a million earth shattering shimmers of,
love and kindness...

The darkness is in my soul,
Will it ever leave me, leave me,
The darkness is taking me whole,
Will it ever leave me, leave me, I just don't know...

The clock ticks, my heart beats, my words are written,
My love is undeniably given.
The gas-lighting has broken me,
I'm trying, trying to bounce back,
You've hurt me so, you've hurt me so...

The darkness is in my soul,
Will it ever leave me, leave me,
The darkness is taking me whole,
Will it ever leave me, leave me, I just don't know...

The empty bed, the cool sheets, the missing warm body
and hands wrapped around me,
Heart-beating broken dreams, the morning chorus, alone,
My heart, forever given, missing him so,
Like the world has caved in on itself...

The darkness is in my soul,
Will it ever leave me, leave me,
The darkness is taking me whole,
Will it ever leave me, leave me, I just don't know…

On the long road to recovery,
Heart wavering doubts,
The kids are sad again,
Will you ever leave us alone,
Will you ever leave our broken dreams…

The darkness is in our soul,
Will it ever leave , leave us,
The darkness is taking us whole,
Will it ever leave us, we just don't know…

Bye Friday

You don't ever imagine that you won't see
your children every day
Do you?
No, you don't!
Unless of some awful heartbreaking tragedy
When some parents lose a child
Unimaginable
Nothing can be worse than that
But this does happen more than we like to think

Life can change in a different way
2.4 family fails
Separation of a different kind
Children are well
But you lose that daily family life
Life becomes disjointed between the two
Nights here
Nights there

Trying hard to keep family life as smooth as possible
Explanations, routines, frustrations and tears
Interspersed with the happiness of a new life
A sense of freedom and domestic calmness
Until it is time to hand them over
The pain, the realisation of the loss you never imagined
Your children's time, is the most precious
I don't want to barter this
I didn't sign up for this kind of mumminess

Resentment rises
Heart's grow heavy
Brains fog
Darkness folds

THAT Friday arrives
That walk to school
Sick to my stomach
Knowing I won't see then until Monday tea
Feels like a lifetime
You may think about the other view
Well, it's said the children are a regret
That they should not have been had

Resentment rises
The hypocrisy of it all kicks in

This is why Bye Fridays are the worst days
I fret about tempers
I mourn
I miss them
I don't want to share my children like this
That's not what I signed up for

Bye Friday!
In fact, Fxck Off Friday!

Trauma bond

'What's the trauma bond?'
I hear you say
'What's the trauma bond?'
I hear you say
I hope you never come across it
Let me explain

The trauma bond is complex
It's full of psyche shit
You think you know what you need to do
But the trauma bond
Conjures a hazy, confusional state
That makes you slip and make mistakes

The trauma bond
Challenges every ounce of emotion
Every memory, every trigger, every family occasion
Maybe it will be OK?
You question your sanity
You question your feelings
You think you've made a mistake
You make errors of judgement
Because you are bonded
Bonded through harm and pain

You think bonded through psychological taunts

What?

So why do you think you are making a mistake?
Because you have been groomed into self-doubt

Groomed into feeling inadequate
Groomed into feeling second best
Groomed into thinking you can't live without them
Groomed into feeling you would be NOTHING without them

You realise this, you feel a fool
You have massaged their ego
You have confused people around you
Until you realise

NO THIS IS NOT WHAT I WANT or MY CHILDREN NEED!

You pick yourself back up
Dust yourself down
And start to move on

They find a new feed immediately
They can't do this alone
You feel pain, anguish, doubt
You think about the loss of the family unit
Have I made a mistake…?

NO!
You have not!

But it hurt the same because you loved them
You allowed them deep into your heart

You allowed them to own you
You now feel discarded even though you were the discarder…
How weird is that?
How difficult to articulate in all honesty
You move on, trying to heal

You move on, finding yourself
Making new friends
Discovering who you are
Enjoying yourself like no time before
Pursuing dreams and love for life
And everything it has to offer

Questions come flooding in
Catching you off guard
Sharing information when you know
This is not a good idea
Why do I do it?
Trauma bond at play, allowing myself to share with them
Who have shared everything
Habit
Suddenly friendliness kicks in
Catches you off guard
Then a request for emotional support comes in
As an empath you respond, a natural instinct
But you know this might backfire

Lies pour out further
You feel a fool
You want the truth

You REACT
Now I am the 'bad one'

I allowed them in again
Under my skin
My thoughts blacken
My thoughts are so dark
I question myself over, over again
My friends see I am now struggling
They reach out
But I have to reach out

And stop this from happening again!

I have learnt another harsh lesson
The trauma bond at play
The empath's nature is a cause of weakness
I need to be aware

Only I can end this
With a little help
From my amazing friends

Shotgun

Shotgun head
Sports day instead
Gish smile
Paper bag head
Split myself in half
Enough said

Alone

A wounded heart
A troubled mind
A need for love
A fear of being alone

Spend time with others
To prevent such muddles
Socialite butterfly
Creating highs

The lows then hit when alone
Immediately sometimes within minutes
Or sometimes days
After leaving

A quandary of sorts:
Welcoming the love
Struggling with the leftovers
It still, always hurts

Part Two
Love & Life

The Phoenix

The phoenix died but rose again,
The ashes warm with amber light,
The cry subsides, a voice is heard,
No more put-downs, no more fights.

No more quips or endless taunts,
Left alone to heal, no haunts,
She hopes, she prays,
That these pains go away,
For those wounds will always,
Sadly remain.

New freedom beckons,
So she reckons,
Of life more simple and pleasant.
Love, laughter, happy-sad ever after,
Is the chapter she is after.

The joy of music, people, writing,
And drama on the bucket list,
There always were twisted jealous pangs,
Insecurities that dampened confidence.

But

The list is strong, no time for deletion,
This list is far, from completion!

Sweet dreams

Once you're a mummy
Life changes forever
Those responsibilities monumentally rise
Your level of protectiveness skyrockets

Your babies, your new love
Your maternal force gigantic
Wherever you go, anticipation is key
Loving, accepting, empathising
Guiding, empowering
And building strength
Is your aim

The end of a day
The night draws close
The babes are settled
They are sleeping

That one last check
That one last sniff of their hair
That one last look of total admiration
Of our precious gems

Sleeping soundly
Looking so peaceful
You could just stay and watch
All night long
Every night the same
But every day even more special than the last

Sweet dreams babies
You are my everything

Autumn vibes

Autumn's here
Another year nearly gone
Autumn's here
Colours changing
Vibrant orange, striking red leaves begin to float aimlessly, gently down
Caramel yellows littering the park as children rush through them
Rustling and squealing with joy; kicking them in the air

A sense of calm and beauty all combined, easing us towards winter
The afternoon autumn sun soothes our skin, squeezing every ray
Before the darker nights set in

Excited children back at school
New-teacher talk quietens down
Halloween chatter begins in the noisy playground

Autumn clothes re-emerge –mustard, burnt orange and browns envelop our soul; comforting, soothing, relaxing –
Bringing peace and gentleness to our hectic lives

Alfresco peters out, we crave warmth from indoors:
Cosiness needed: patio heaters just don't cut it
Cups of soup, cocoa. Hearty vegetable squash soup stew with courgette dumplings. If you haven't tried you should

Winter planning begins. Such anticipation for Christmas so soon, too soon, let's wait a while
Let's enjoy the beautiful, cooler, calmer autumnal days
Let's slow down, put the brakes on and imagine
We are those leaves finding their footing grounding us for the next season

Autumn vibes - stay awhile

London bound

We're on a train, London-bound
The kids and I, listening for sounds
The beep, beep, beep
The whoosh and the swoosh
And away we go

We're on a train to London
The kids, aww, what wonder!
The giggles and the smiles
We talk to all, within a mile

The chatting and the gazing
Seems all just so amazing
Our train bound for London
Who will we meet today?

A musician, a gentleman, a market trader
A kind fellow parent and a friendly waiter
All going about their world
Looking out for others

A heart full of sorrow
Triggers days bright for the morrow
The faith in man, in humanity
Redeemed in the big city

We're on a train, London-bound
There are certainly more sounds
Welcoming, laughing, singing and playing
All this life keeps on swaying

Life is a changing
Life is awakening
Life has only just begun
Let it rise so beautiful

Under the afternoon sun

The end is near

The end is near
It arrives so hastily
Fast and furious
Ever so quickly

The rush the push
The crush of the crowds
Spending and spending money
They haven't got

In a consumer world
With an obsession of materialism
We succumb to greed
Rather than those that need a feed

Where those who have,
have more than they will ever need
And those that with nothing
Look on to their nothingness
When a world could be so different
Where the rich could help the poor

And those who have everything
Those that have no idea
Of the challenges some face
On an hour-to-hour basis
Those who have everything
Will sadly never see those good people
Who struggle

They don't exist you see
It's far too inconvenient to think otherwise
Their moral compass can't be challenged
No, they mustn't have to think
About AN Other

Where those who have,
Have more than they will ever need
And those with nothingness
Look upon their nothingness
With a heart-rendering plea
Their cries go unheard

It's Christmastime
We must be festive and jolly
Not humbug and glum
But this time isn't easy
For those in greatest need

What I ask of every one of you
Is think of AN Other
And do something for those with nothing
Not lip service
Not something for social media status
But get your hands stuck right in
And spend some time
In the nothingness
You might be surprised
By the love you'll find there

Best friend

What would I do without you in my life?
You are always here
Listening
Checking in
Supporting
Loving me

What would I do without you in my life?
You are always here
Reassuring me things will get easier
That new life has begun
A new chapter spills open

What would I do without you in my life?
You are always here
Those dark days
Those dark nights
Those thoughts I wasn't gonna make it through
You were there, always helping me just be
Be calm, go steady,
Breathe Amanda, just breathe

What would I do without you in my life
You are always here
2 years nearly has flown by
You've been here with me through change
Never faltering
Always calm
What would you like to do, you ask

Be creative
Then do it, you say

What would I do without you in my life?
You are always here
A rock
A confidante
A true friend
You make me hear music
You make me see the flowers
You make me see the beauty in the darkness
The sunshine in the gloom
The bright skies in the brain fog

What would I do without you in my life?
You are always here
When I am being daft
When I need a telling-off
When I'm being ridiculously paranoid
You are here
I feel I don't deserve your friendship
When I'm like that

What would I do without you in my life?
You are always here
I am thankful for your friendship
I am joyful of the creativity in my life
I am healing as you hold my hand
My dear friend, I love you so.
You are the shining moon amongst the darkness of my days
You saved me
Thank you x

Feline company

Just me and the Bengal boys this weekend
Home so quiet
Empty children's bedrooms
The boys wander looking for them
Automatic bedtime checks
Empty beds

Constant hunger
Meowing
You've just been fed boys
You guys bored?!

We all wander in and out the rooms
Wondering why time goes so slowly
Not all the time
Plenty to do
Jobs at home
Planning for the babes

There is meeting friends
Playing bass
Practising dance
Writing about life
Reading
Resting (find that one the hardest)
Watching TV – just not me
Could be doing a job…
But I'm tired
I need to rest, recuperate and have some rehab

This weekend I've done that
I've seen a few friends
I've played some music
I've read my book
I've watched a few episodes of Mrs Maisel
I've done jobs
I've rested more

So there, I have had the quietest weekend
Solo on record
I've done it, it was OK, maybe not as hard

It's so quiet though
And the time does go slowly
Snail like
But they will be home soon

Love me like this

Someone to hold me
Someone to care
Someone to guide me
When I am scared

Someone to love me
Someone to ravish me
Someone to gig with
When life seems so bare

Someone to laugh with
Someone to cuddle me
Someone to play scrabble
and avoid the rabble with

Someone to treat me
Someone to meet
Someone to drink espresso with
and eat cherry gelato

Someone to play
and listen to music with
Someone to walk by my side
On a beach
In a wood
On a street
In a faraway town
In a different world
Where I can be with you

Are you the one for me?
Will I find this someone?
Is this someone found?
I do not know

Someone, somewhere
Somebody, somehow

Please

Love me like this

Camping bliss

Outdoor fun
Outdoor freedom
Whilst others it's a prison
Outdoor brain
White and grey matter relax
The mind and soul in a combined escape, hatched

To leave the world of work and frazzled times behind
To allow the cortex to rest, recoup, and rewind
To rest a while... for a while
At least
Before we reface the beast

The treadmill
The hamster wheel
The Swiss cheese hole marathon
The epic roundabout of busy life
Of our speedway of modern life

It's not for some
It is for us
We still do gadgetise – (is that even a word?!)

We feel free
We collect wood
We forage
We play cards
We play board games
We tell stories
We toast marshmallows

We are free
We are free from life's strife
We are mentally and physically untied
We don't need to hide here
We are safe
We are on our own
We did this all on our own

Self-reliant, empowered and feeling higher
Feeling stronger on our return
From camping bliss

7 nights 7 days

So now you've both gone
My heart feels numb
7 nights
7 days
My life a haze, a hum of existence

So now you've both gone
I'm frightened of the journey
The weather, the anger
The actions of that other

So now the nest is empty for a while
My feelings surmount all this time
Of wondering and hoping
And a legacy of coping

The love of children
Most powerful
Uncontrollably attached
Forever, in my heart
A 100% match

Feelings of powerlessness
Taking over my mind
Consuming me whole
Don't go down that black hole

7 days
7 nights

The longest yet
I cannot not fret
Of *what ifs* and *buts* and a cascade of memories
Of a previous canvas that was let

So now you're gone
Time for distraction
Try not to reflect too deep
Catastrophise not

7 days
7 nights
Is really not that long

Bot life

I want to be able to talk to a person
Is that too hard?
I want to check my groceries with a real-life person
Is that too hard?
I want to talk to a human when I call a company
Is that too hard?
I want to speak with a real fucking person
Why is that so hard!

Take your bots and your contactless nonsense far away
We don't need this auto robotic let's not use our brain life
Where children will not learn how to handle money
Where teenagers live in their bedrooms unable to talk to a real person
Where social media robs society of real relationships
Where social media causes anxiety and depression
Where boys and girls are over-sexualised, strutting around with their prepubescent bodies looking like 18-year-olds

Where TikTok, Insta, Facebook promote a vehicle for perfected lives and bodies
Where eating disorders are tenfold and are promoted to drive traffic
Where all this shit manifests as normalised
Where conversations overheard by Facebook suddenly pop up suggesting identical matches. How can Facebook know?
Can they hear you? Can they read this?

Of course
I'm a mug like the rest
A sheep, but not quite a follower
A black sheep witnessing this shit storm about to unfold
Where human brain thought will no longer exist
Where I am also to blame like everyone else
Stop following
Wake up

Get me off this railroad life

Get me off this railroad life
A kaleidoscope of chaos
Of blinkered thinkers
And some rotten stinkers

This life is derailed
The train has departed
Is it too late?
No, let's start a new rail

Where people are loved
Where people are cherished
Not used, abused, and misused
To suit their muse

An inclusive life of equality and facts
Not being marshmallowed to wear ridiculous hats

Not a jester, not a clown or a puppet on a string
Let there be no master who tightly pulls those strings

Do not be choked, but breathe deeply my friend
Stay calm
Ride the storm
It's societal norms we're rejecting

Hope

A new morning awakens
Sun rising lazily
But, it's there
It's present
It's begun?
There's no sign of it breaking

Another day but this one's different
There's a sweet smell
A friendliness about the air
There's no indifference

Sunlight catches the fairy dancer
The delight of children's smiles
Chasing the prism light
A sun dance whilst children prance

There's that light again
It's tough and tenacious
That light, that energy
Cannot be put out
So, refrain, just refrain

Shine brightly sun
Shine on through our hearts
Shine on our friendships
And let hope into our lives
Our muse
Our love
And find it's sister, peace
Together
Without one, we will not find the other

Lover

A new lover's gaze
In that misty morning craze
The morning after
Calmness ensues

A shy little peek under the covers
You're both naked
Sweaty
Relaxed

The first walk to the bathroom
Tattooed ass on show
The sun is shining through
No time for blushing

Love has been made
Passion unfolded
Beautifully expressed
Amongst the constant caress

The night becomes the morning,
Morning becomes the afternoon
Talking, laughing, making love
Reflecting on what happened here
On that delightful night

It felt right

A solitary cigarette on Christmas Day

A solitary cigarette on Christmas Day
A stark change
Realisation of what's gone before

This time I stand
Relaxed, naughty
Reflecting on the most beautiful day, there was

A sharp intake of breath
Taking in fresh air
Not controlled
Or contrived
But free as the bat floating in the wind before me

A solitary cigarette
One child asleep
One chatting
Boys talk
Airing the thoughts and minds alike

Relaxed
Blackness of the garden
But the blackness is golden
Shining strong
Like the beautiful stars my loves are

An epitiomy of perfection
Which is so obscure and unimaginable
This day, this night
In whatever
Way
Is the imperfection
Perfection
I'm craving for

New Year

A New Year beckons
The sky is bright blue this morning
The sun shining high amongst the Humber Estuary
The bridge, a magnificent structure gleaming in the sun
It's lasted another year
Some of us have made it through the year
Some of us sadly not

The roads are quiet
Revellers are now sleeping
The early-nighters are bright-eyed and out walking
Reflections come through with tidal force and momentum
Happy New Year
All the Best to You
Floating through the ether like fishes swimming with the shoal

Excitement, resolutions, no resolutions, hopes, and planning begin
We need some structure to our world
Something to look forward to
Maybe a realistic goal
Or just no pressure
No pressure
At all
Allow that balloon to deflate, relax
Just being in whatever moment comes along
Maybe that's all we need

The world ails so painfully
Like a wounded animal

So much suffering to so many
How do we deal with that
How do we get on with our lives
Ignorance?
Denial?
Want?
Kindness?
Love?
Life is a complicated jigsaw, a modern tapestry of life

It's a new year
There's Veganuary
There's Dry January
There's Detox January
There's Stop Smoking January
There's Diet January
The list goes on –
Take it easy
Nothing is achieved quickly
No pressure
No pressure at all

It's New Year
Life can be and is so incredibly short
Enjoy your own company
Enjoy the company of others
Enjoy the company of strangers
Enjoy those precious moments with whom you love
Share kindness and love, we can try to make the world
A more peaceful and forgiving place

We are all in this together
We always have been
We always will be

Shining through

The light penetrates the room
Bright, happy, sun shining leading the light
of this beautiful morning
Flowing like honey

Oberon meows
This home awakens
Patter of feet
The princess emerges
Smiling like a beautiful butterfly
gliding on the soft breeze

Morning snuggles
Marcello deafens us all
With his hungry yowl
The prince comes through, the sun
lightening his Samson locks –
What's all the noise?

It's only 6.51 mum
I know
The cats have meowed, the girl awake
I'm now up
Tell me about it, Son!

Guinea pigs wheeking
The menagerie at full complement
Everyone's hungry
Everyone's chattering

Good morning!

Superego man

Superego
Superego
Betcha wanna go go!
With your glitzy jacket
and your wham bam woman
You think you can have anyone!

Superego
Superego
Betcha wanna go go!
With your cock you
think you can have a go!

Superego
Superego
Betcha wanna go go!
With your beer belly girth
You're the one giving birth

Superego
Superego
Betcha wanna cum and go
With your alter-ego in tow

Superego
Superego
I'm tired of your calls
Just shut the fuck up and grow some balls!

What are you thinking?

What are you thinking?
I do not know
Will I ever
I suspect that's 'no'

What are you thinking?
I do not know
Of days like this
That just grow and grow?

Of moments of plenty
I cast my role
That's maybe not fruitful
Maybe not worthy

I drop the guard
The barrier
The layer of protectiveness
And succumb to the journey
That ignites in me

A fraction of a heart

Where a fraction determines your progress
How can a fraction of heart matter so much?
Affecting treatments, access – guides to be cared by
Where a fraction determines your emotional love
How can this fraction matter so much?
Affecting relations, choices and preferences we make?
Fractions of blood being ejected, reduced or preserved
Fractions of emotions being received or rejected
These delicate blood flows
These delicate feelings of the heart
In need of nourishment and fulfilment
Let them be allowed to flow

The flow is the central core of our inner being
and our heart muscle.
Let it be as strong and if it cannot be strong,
then allow it to be cared for
and strengthened through LOVE.

Brown eyes

Brown eyes
Caramel richness
Flowing like warm chocolate velvet
Spilling over into an open heart

Brown eyes
Always the same
What is it with brown eyes
Which makes my heart remain?

Remain so entangled
Interwoven
Happily
Within layers of soft gestures and kindness
So comforting

Brown eyes
Full of mysterious life
An adventurous spirit
What must it be like to be your wife

A soft, delicate nature
Wrapped with a darkness that is beautiful
So beautiful that you'd drown in the sea
Of that brown-eyed handsome man

Brown eyes
Your eyes are so deep
Deep enough to find the bottom of the ocean
Within the abyss layer
There are twinkling lights in and amongst
That light that shines through the darkness
Which envelopes us forever

Half moon

Oh, so beautiful
So translucent and fluffy
Like marshmallow hearts
Nestling amongst lovers

Half Moon
Are you half-hearted
Or in for the whole existential existence
Are you fickle and bottomless
Like a prosecco lunch

Oh, Half Moon
I see you pondering on the night, then the day
On a clear day, you never hide
Crisp and clear like morning dew on grass
And in cloud, you hide away

Oh, Half Moon
Thinking so deep
Can your words of wisdom
Fulfil my void of sleep
I just can't count any more sheep

Oh, Half moon
Look at your beauty
Your wit and your prominence
I hope you stay a while longer
In your sheer luminance

Lovers in the moonlight

The moonshine glows silky
against our bodies
The opalescent light shines on the water's edge
creating dancing reflections
The air is cool and clear
woodsmoke lingers on our hair and clothes
Pupils adjusting to the darkness of the woodlands

Deeper, deeper we go
The grass, moist and uneven
A snake glides
Grass gymnastics like dragonflies
dart excitedly searching for one another
Wantonness, love, gentleness, and lust

A call from a bird
A conversation travelling through the air
Feeling free amongst nature touching our bodies
We are simply alive

Busy minds
Busy thoughts
Not now
Rest awhile
Seeking pleasure for one another
Always in our minds

The night growing late
The blue moon rising higher
The beauty of all this mesmerising
The climax teasing and satisfying

Hand in hand
Shoulder to shoulder
Step by step
Guided by the natural light
out of the woods
into the night
To sleep side by side
amongst the stars

Random tears

Off guard they catch you
Hot flowing down your blushered cheeks
Like a cleansing of a soul
An astringent wake-up call

Independence pinches
your conscience
The tears still raining down
into insignificance

Looking in the mirror
Who do you see
No more fragile girl
staring back at me

Those eyes of tears
That carry so much emotion
Restless, tired
sensitive and loving

Ready to give a little bit more
Ready to be loved
Ready to have fun
Ready to be held a little while longer

Shining

Azure blue skies
Magnificent sun
How powerful you are
Radiating down

On our naked bodies
Soaking every ray
Soothing every bone
Calming our souls

Relaxation kicks in
The mind wanders
From the complex
To one of pleasure

How quiet the sound around
Dampened, tranquil
Faint intermittent chatter
The brain brake is on

Life slows down
Welcoming rest
No need to rush
Pause a while, my friend

Heart sparks

Heart sparks chaos
Heart pounding
Breathtaking
Heart eating gulps
Engulfs the evening

Children bathing
Mother saying,
"Can you get yourselves dry,
I need to call for help babes,
Mummy's heart's racing."

"What, are you going to die?"
"Doubt it, I know what it is son and know what I need,
All will be fine, just need medicine,
Can you help your little sister get dressed."
"Of course, Mummy."

Heart's beating fast
Chest flickering
Anxiety rising
Trying to keep cool
No one picks the phone up
Gotta get the kids cared for
Over-thinking now

Irregular irregularly beating
Atria in chaos

Pacemaker overridden
Electrics misfire
Too many cooks
The broth is overflowing

Heart sparks chaos
Feeling woozy
Feeling sick
I've been taking too much stick
And I've now got sick

Nurse gets her own medicine
Frightened
Intravenous drug
Need it
But will I react OK?
It takes a while
Riddled with nerves

Monitors beeping
Nurse radar on full max
Some are Tachy
Some are Brady
Can't switch off
Bleep bleep bleeping

Somersault of sparks
The magic mix
The concoction
Conduction is restored
Sinus rhythm is the new song

Sparks fly
Heart's troubles
Are mended
Brain keeps hearing beeps
Quieter they will become

Time to move on
A blip in time
A wake-up call
I am not invincible

I am human
I am Mandy
It's time to reflect...

I want to start a rebellion

I want to start a rebellion
Where the rebels rebel
Freely with their own minds
So that everyone can tell

I want to start a rebellion
Whatever age, to speak and tell
Of the untruths and the truths
Of those misleading mouths

I want to start a rebellion
Who stand up for others
Of the rules and the regulations
That constrict and restricts people's life

I want to start a rebellion
Because no one's fucking hearing
The far cries of society
In the need for active listening

I want to start a rebellion
Because I don't want this for my kids
My kids want a rebellion
We're ready for this fight

Lying here with you

Mummy and daughter
Woman and little girl
Connected forever
Always intertwined

Lying side by side
Some nights when she needs me
Snuggled in close
Always skin-to-skin

Her warm feet prodding my legs
Her little heart beating
Her sniffles, her coughs
Her sleep breathing
Her presence resounding

Sleeping soundly
Hand reaches out
To find me
Is mummy there?
Always needs to know
The continued umbilicus
In the big wide world

Lying here with you

Sober sex

The lights are on dimly
The candles are burning
Enough light to see the beauty unfold
Excitement rising

A little wine
Helping the boldness
Perhaps
No wine needed
Perhaps

It's daylight
Sunshine pouring in across
the vibrant sheets
Sleepy eyes looking
Reflecting
Smiling
Needing a cup of tea

But no, no tea yet
It's not time for that
Gazing onwards
Those horny thoughts not yet done

A trembling heart
Spilling out
Hands are grabbed
Legs intertwined
No wine needed

Sober sex
Sober lovemaking
Sober fucking
Boldness erect
Completes the morning set

A strength of champions
No dim light
No wine
Just oxytocin
Enveloping the souls within

The joy of laughing

Laughing, giggling, smiling, and teasing
Spending time with you ever-so-pleasing
You make me laugh like I have
not laughed in years
So funny and chatty
and equally batty

What a joy to spend time
That flies by hour after hour
Thinking and looking
Reflecting on the hours

An instant rapport
A different outlook on life
Laughing
Laughing so much
about everything!

You make me laugh

You make me laugh
You make me laugh so much
That my eyes water
Streaming joy down my face

You make me giggle
You make me smile
You rub out my niggles
And make me wiggle

You make me laugh
When I need it most
Creating warmth inside me
My dear friend

Chaos of kite

Her tousled hair amongst the tightening kite

Amongst the buffeting wind through the cumulous cloud

Free as a bird they fly together, weaving in and out, avoiding calamity

Signifying a journey anyone can take to avoid societal woe

Frisky

Hot sun
Evokes passion
Sensual soothing fire in our bodies
Connected and intertwined

Sweat pouring down in-between legs
Breathing hard
Deeply now
Catching our breath

Rolling in the grass
Not a care in the world
Tension rising
Sun, burning hot

It's time to go now
One last embrace
One last kiss
Before we go our separate ways

Let's go camping

Let's go camping
Fresh air
Freedom
Field love
Free from modern farce

Let's go camping
Tranquility
Trust
Trees
Translocated from suburban towns

Let's go camping
Cook on fire
Chat about life
Care for our surroundings
Concrete jungle left behind

Let's go camping
Where they bring no social boundaries
Where they scream and prance half the night
Where they lack self-dignity

Let's go camping
To listen to TVs blaring
To listen to incessant tuneless nonsense
To see their antics whilst children try to sleep late at night

Let's go camping
Freaking barking dogs
Foolish owners who seem oblivious
Framed and scattered with bright LED lights

Let's give up camping, then?
Let's ignore that then?
Look, that's not the way
Lacking social boundaries nothing is learnt
respectability will be lost if silence remains

Let's keep camping
Share some decorum
Share kindness, consideration and etiquette
Share never give up

"Just show them the decent way"

Red sky

Red Sky at Sunset
Dust particle madness
Pressure is high
But it shall be a better day tomorrow

Red sky at night
If only I had some Turkish Delight
Tonight
Right now
Right here
It soothes me so

Red sky over the Humber bridge
Amongst potato cloud fluff
My body, my mind hurts
Hoping I can find some respite
Maybe, a lucky sprite
Who takes me under their wing

Red sky, so enriching, a vibrant energy
Exhaustion kicks in
Take me to sleep on red sky
Where I will sleep soundly
and safely in your arms

Social butterfly

Two souls
Two minds
Two hearts
What a social lark

Two empaths
Fragile, but strong with a firm path
who always laugh
It really doesn't matter about the past

A love for people
A zest for life
Creative minds that can think alike
amongst the craziness of life

Self-reflectors,
Adjusting all the time
To changes between self and society
through humbleness, not piety

Sometimes extrovert butterflies
amongst the crowds
But sometimes introvert
with the need for time alone

A paradox of people craving solitude
A need for time and balance from the traumas of life
As these two beings deserve no more strife
But simply a beautiful life

Blue moon

Once in a Blue Moon
Blue by name, not colour
Thirteen months have passed
Coinciding with another

A saying we know
But how many know the meaning?
A rarity
A moon shining bright into the night

Camping view
Rising over the woods higher and higher
Boasting itself boldly and beautifully
Illuminating the grasslands below

Children could play in the moonlight
Lovers can embrace and gaze
Calling out loud as owls twit-twoo
Such a cacophony of sound

Moonlight madness
Lunacy
Perceptually
Ravenously
Perhaps, just once in a Blue Moon

Cherub

Beautiful golden curly locks
Cheeky smile beaming
Soft cherry lips perfectly pursed
sitting there, pen in hand

Piercing blue eyes
A stare not to be reckoned with
One fleeting wrong step
You will certainly regret

Drawing, painting, making, and doing
A haven and founder of creativity
Pipe cleaners, papier-mache, bio glitter and glue
Making sometimes a magnificent poo!

Relaxing, doing her thing
A Zen activity, flying on her wings
To a magical place where her brain can be free
To be who she wants to BE

No traps, no snares of tablet life
No screens and memes
Or uncomfortable strife
No digital locusts swarming my child
Filling her head with utter non SENSE

So, leave her be with her beads and ribbons
Leave her be with her buttons and lolly sticks
Leave her be with her sticks, sand, and stones
Leave her be with her flowers, weeds, and bees
Leave her be with her vegetable beds

Above all, let her use her head

Fucking hormones

A torrid cycle of doom and woe
An energy blast that doesn't last
A fleeting thrill here and there
Just wanting to rest my head here

A raging tornado,
A whirlwind of doubt
Sucks your working day
Fast

Barely keeping your eyes open
You plod through the day
Anxious if someone can see
That fragile shell

Your cam is off
The pitch is slow
You dread the communication
You just want to go
Your confidence low

Children time
You force a smile
You fake your time
Trying to normalise

Comes to bedtime
Desperate to sleep
But you need to unwind

A little
So you try and play
You try and read
You try and write
It shouldn't be a fight

The self-loathing comes
The critical self
Of this body, this vessel
This mind

The mind flips back
Like a chapter in a book
A stormy sea
Waiting for the waves to calm
The cycle to calm

Until next month
You fucking hormones
Just leave me alone

New love

New love
Striking you between the eyes
Cupid's arrow caught you off guard
Barriers down
You snook in there

How did that happen
I do not know
Wounded
Hurt before
Staring across the foreshore

Triggers alerted
Heart races
Brain collides inside
You feel vulnerable
You are unsure

Confused, but enjoying the delight
of a new encounter that seems
To grow bigger and stronger
But you're terrified
of rejection

So does it stop
No, because it feels so good
It feels right
It feels enjoyably terrifying
But it's a risk to the heart and mind

Life is for living and loving
Not for hiding
Caution is good
Let's linger here longer my love

Seaweed life

Salty seaweed
Entangled around toes
Wrapped inside and outside
with love for the soul

Green, brown, and red leaves
Bubbling with beads
Full of spiders, apparently
ready to spawn!

All toed together
Spiders welcomed
Holistic, magic
Bumps, warts, and all

Squidgy, slimy, kelpy and tasty,
Now, now! Don't be hasty!
Don't knock it, till you've tried it
You may just like it!

Salty seaweed
Such a delicacy inside and out
Enriching minds and bodies
for centuries forever

Something silly

Something silly he said
Tezza Nova
Is he Casanova?
Or a dog called Rover?

Something silly he said
Mandy Pandy
Ooh, she's sweet as candy!
Or is that randy?

Something silly he said
For Speak Out Scunny
Whilst I'm lying here
Sunbathing in honey

Something silly he said
From Lanzarote
Gorging on fruits
Sunbathing her botty

Something silly he said
For the Chara banc from Hull
Who as you know
Are always on the pull

Something silly he said
Now this is getting weary
The tedious rhyming
And Mandy ain't even leary!

You see

You see this woman
You see this mother
You see the fragile girl within
Who hasn't healed enough

You see her love
You see her passion
You see her creativity
You see her zest for life

You see her bubbly-ness
You see her drive forward
Taking new challenges as they arrive
But, she hasn't healed enough

You see her cry
You see her tear herself to shreds
You see her lose her voice
She is still healing, you see

You see her love others
You see her help others
You see her prioritise others
Whilst she let's her brain-rot fester

You see that you love her
She sees she loves you
You hear her say 'leave me' and
'I am no good'
You say you're not going anywhere

You see how hurt this human girl is
Picking up the pieces and boldly moving forward
She wavers, she panics, she can't breathe
You say, everything will be OK

You see she thinks
You see she ponders on all of this
You see her brain fight and her heart pound
You offer her light in the shadows
She wants to believe it will all be OK

You can show how she can see more clearly
You can show her how to love and be loved

120 seconds

Mum, Mum, Muum!!!
Yeah, I'm here, I'm in the other room
Ohh yeah, can I have a drink please?
I'm hungry, I need some food too
Can you play a game with me, now?
Hang on a minute

Mum, Mum, Muuum!
Where are you, I can't find you
I'm in the loo, having a wee
Oh yeah, mum, can you get me a game down please?
Yeah, I'm having a wee, in a minute!

Mum, mum, muuuum!
Yeah, what now love? I'm having a pee
Can I have something to eat?
Yeah, in a minute, I'm having a pee
Mum, mum, muuuuuum, you're taking years in there, when Will you come out?
Yeah, I'm peeing like a racing car, I won't be long!

Mum, Muuum, muuuum!
Oh my goodness, yes what is it?
Will we go on holiday this year?
Okay, so which thing do you need right now?
Mmmm, mum, can we have waffles for breakfast Tomorrow?!

Step in my shoes

Step in my shoes
Step in my shoes just for one day
Step in my shoes
Step in my shoes just for one morning
Step in my shoes
Step in my shoes just for one hour

Just to see what it's like
How hard it is to get through a school day
Where your autistic brain
Fears every part of the school day,
Where your brain fires randomly
And impulsively because your cup
is overflowing

Just see what it's like
To deal with friends goading you,
Teasing you, telling you to do things
Then get all the blame

Just see what it's like
When you are not understood
When you don't have the support
When there isn't the understanding
When you're avoided
When walking to school

Just see what it's like
When you are labelled –

Naughty
Spoilt
Rude
Crazy
Parents fault
Weird
Freak

How would you feel if this were your child
Critical parents who judge
Assume, presume?
Shake their heads?
Who tut?
Who ignore?
Who stare?
And JUDGE in your little
'Perfect' cliques
Snooping on social media
But never speak...
Who do you think you are?!

You have no idea, what it's like
To walk in my son's shoes

You have no idea what it's like
To walk in my shoes, as his mother

You have no idea the lengths gone
To help my child, learn everything
To be the best parent I can be

Before you gossip, before you judge
Just think about this 8-year-old child
Who is struggling so much

That his brain goes into meltdown

Just think about this 8-year-old
Who has thought about ending
His own life not that long ago

Just think about this 8-year-old boy
Who tries hard to be 'socially acceptable'

Just think about that, please show compassion

And if you ever have questions
Or something you don't understand
About my son, then please

Come to me
Come to me

Talk to me

Pyjamas

A pair of tartan pyjamas neatly
folded on the bedhead
Looking on, it makes me smile
to see them next to mine

Sometimes here
Sometimes there
But, forever in my heart;
Nothing smarts

It's as if you're here, when you're there
When you're there, you are here!
It doesn't matter which sphere
Because you're always here!

Side by side
A tartan floral team
A kaleidoscope of colour
Sends vibrancy through my eyes
and ears

So when I'm lying here alone
You're still next to me
Always, I hope
Thinking of when we'll wear our pyjamas
again!

When you think you'll never

When you think you'll never
love again
Bruised, battered
with worn out hope

One day comes, you're raw with fear
You want to love
be loved
Even though you're bruised and battered with fragile hope

Be bold and brave
Come on, keep the hold
of gentleness
But, cautiously live with hope

Steady now
It's fine, be slow
No one knows how
This is no game-show

When you think you'll never
love again
Where self-protect mode is in force
and cupid strikes that rusty arrow

Where love's speared inside
and two gentle hearts collide
Where love is present
once again

When you think you'll never
love again
Just take some time, pause a while
And
Don't lose hope!

My perfect place

A place of love
Of genuine hearts
A place of adventure
Nestled within the humdrum
Where tenacity's legend

Introverted cells
Extroverted membranes
Ambiverted tangling
Retroverted souls
Finding peace in other's engines

Perfection is a myth
Gratitude is a gem
Amongst the rubble
Holding the stem
Wilting here and there, because that's not perfection

A perfect place?
Why, there isn't one
It's where your heart lies most
Allow your heart to settle
You will find yourself, I hope

A place of forgiveness
Compassion for self
And one another
Life's short on many levels
Make every day, always matter

Strangled by words

Strangled by words
At the throat
Croaking
Deep breathed
Constrained
It's just not worth the reply
to this bombastic fictitious hierarchy
Restrained

The irony
Freed by words
OUT LOUD
breathing freely
without constriction
allowing recollection
For my mind's depiction

Frozen webs

Silky webs
Intricate
Such fragility
Like the human mind

But who are these creatures that
weave complex intelligent threads
of beauty and vulnerability
as frozen white sculptures

Delicate spiders
Oh, how so small
Oh, how so big humans are
Could we create this magnificent home
so easily?

These spookily creations
wrapped around children's playgrounds, logs, trees, leaves
for us to see
Strong but weak
Weak but strong
In the spider's world
Is this more magnificent?

Spooky tardiness or winter solstice
I think it is

Snowfall

Sleepy eyes waking
The sandman dust visible in the mirror
A glint of whiteness catches the eye
No, it's not, has it?

Looking further at the frosted glass, everything's white
I smile
It's snowed!

I want to yell excitedly to the children
"Darlings it's snowed, look out your windows"
Oh - there not here, you remember
A tide of tears feeling tsunami like impending

No, it's OK
When they wake in those beds elsewhere
They will smile, shout, squeel with delight
They will run barefoot outside because that's we did last, maybe
I think on that
This makes me smile

I say outloud,
"The kids are going to be so excited this morning!"
I walk back to bed,
Snuggling back down
Everything's fine

Whenever, wherever with whomever
It ignites the child within us all
Every time
That majestic snow falls

The life to come?

What's happened to human life
AI now incredibly rife
Alexa, Siri, Alpha and Celeste
Taking over your brain
Creating, an incoming reign

A world where you don't think
Without causing a stink
It's the new norm
Do you see the almighty storm?

A world of corporate coercion
Where there's no societal cohesion
To make us believe we're smarter than ever
Oh, aren't we so clever!

A pat on the back
Not an eyebrow is raised
Have you used GPT chat
No, I've used my fucking brain

A world of no waiter's
No check out staff
No radio presenters
Coz we have Charlie bot

Now, now don't be a hater

Where children are told to learn online
Where bookclubs and libraries are seen as slime
Where everything normal

Is deemed to be paranormal

I am glad I'm not younger
I hope, life doesn't go under

Political conditioning
For the capitalist giants
Just stop, and think
When you ask a question
Who's fuelling the answers?

I have done...

I have done many things right
But, I have done many things wrong
The mental plight can be fraught
Doing what we think, we ought

I have done many things badly
But, I have done many things well
The unsurmountable feeling
Why, that makes my heart swell

I have said the wrong thing
But, I have said some right things
Life, a balance of ports
Amongst a selection, of liquorice alsorts

I have said bitter words
But, I have said sweet words
Forcing away the herd
Towards words and worlds less absurd

I keep going; trying to be positive
Life, can take many hostages
I keep going, because I am doing my best
It's rather cold today, but I'll wear my *girl vest*

Paradoxical beings

Para Para Para
doxically
Life is
Emotions are and
emotions aren't

Paradoxically,
We like and we don't like
those shadows of the night
because, sometimes they help us,
but sometimes they hinder

A parody of paradoxes
Where they swoop in and amongst
Neither right or deemed wrong
Whismical, like a cheap thong

The greatest paradox..
Is our own minds
Juggling, flexing and much romancing
Fearful that our hearts will be left, behind

Para Para Para
doxically
Without a paradox
Who are we!
Do we even know?
Unless Tezza sez so!

Missing you

Lying here tonight
Imagining your arms around me tightly
enveloping my soul
feeling the warmth of your soul
rather than staring down that rabbit hole

Ray's Poem

If I could only

If I could only speak to you
these last two years have been rough

If I only could speak to you for a moment
it would be worth a billion
in these crazy times in Brough

If I could only run some things by you
that you will be disappointed
but not surprised to hear
It's been unrelenting trauma to everyone's ears

If I could only hear your voice
and words of wisdom
To me, to all
It would make these issues seem small

If I could see your smile
If you could see your grandson and meet your
granddaughter for the first time
This would make you and me smile

Your calming presence
Your balanced view
Your friendliness to all
Your festive cheer
Reminds me of yesterday year

If I could only hear your voice
Outloud, once more
But, its not so bleak
Because you have always been here
I just didn't see
Remarkably
Clear
You
Are
Here
In
My mind
My heart
And still talking to me
It's not so bleak
Ray's always here

Acknowledgements

It has to be acknowledged that the last 2 years have been challenging. What was a positive change in circumstances came at a great cost to my mental health and well-being, but a move that was right for my children and my own sanity.

I have so many friends and family members that have unrelentingly shown support, loved me when I could not love myself, checked in on me during those darker times and for that I am forever in your debt.

Thank you from the bottom of my heart to:
My children, my mother Chris, Samantha, Dean, Charlotte, Peter, Steve, Claire, Jackson D, Liz, Gary, Keith, Kavita, Andrew, Stacey, Gemma, Sharon, Michelle, Terry & Coleen G, Sally, Sally H, Sam N, Sue, Alex, John U, Tracy, Staci, Kayleigh, Karen, Zach, Ellie, Hunni, John, Patrick, Helen, Hannah, Lynne, Helen G, Christopher, Hollie, Parmeet, Sarah S and all my creative friends and Facebook community.

A special thanks to Sarah Drury for her encouragement, support and feedback.

Thank you to Peter and Geoff for their kind words.

Last, but by no means least: to Terry who has shown me how love can be loved again and in the most beautiful and healthy way.

Amanda Crundall

Amanda began to write again in January 2022 after her friends urged her to write down how she was feeling as a therapeutic outlet; so she did. She has rediscovered her creative self, amongst being a busy mummy and working life. Amanda works as a full time heart failure nurse specialist and is a single mother to two amazing children. Surprising many of her friends how she finds the time amongst such a busy life remains her best kept secret.

You can find Amanda performing at her local spoken word events at Speak Out Scunny, The Confessional, Away with Words. Her debut performance was at Yada Yada Noise in February 2022 to whom she is more than grateful to; a special shout out to Alice & Mickey. She now proudly co-hosts 'Rabbiting On' spoken word group held at 'The Rabbit Hole' Independent bookshop, Brigg alongside poetry babe and partner in poetry Amy Garratt. Her poetry was featured in The Scroll Magazine during October 2022.

In 2023, Amanda performed her poetry at The Festival of Love, D31 Art Gallery, Doncaster and Scunthorpe Pride on behalf of the Speak Out Scunny. She co hosted the spoken word stage at the No Limits Festival 2023 held at Normanby Hall, Scunthorpe.

More recently, Amanda has taken to the radio waves and has featured both pre-recorded and 'live on air' for Phoenix Community Radio, Goole.

Without this outlet and the support of friends and family, life would be a much darker place. This is her debut publication.

Contact details:
Email: Shewearsherheartonhersleeve@proton.me
Facebook: 'She wears her heart on her sleeve'
Twitter (X): Heartsleeve2024
Instagram: @AmandaCrundallPoet
YouTube: @MandyCrundall

WATCH HERE: